Viking Bookkeeping Page

Chapter 1:

Intro to Bookkeeping

Not everyone who has a great business idea has been to business school. If you're just starting out in the business world, the financial side of your new company can seem daunting. This book will show you how to navigate bookkeeping options and choose the one that will best suit your small business.

Bookkeeping is a vital component of any business, and getting it right from the very beginning will prevent problems in the future. You should organize your bookkeeping as soon as you can to maximize efficiency and give your business an organizational boost.

The first thing to understand if you're going to do your own bookkeeping is the difference between bookkeeping and accounting. If you're unfamiliar with these practices, you'd be forgiven for thinking they're the same thing. Many seasoned business people would struggle to put the distinction between them into words. Before you look into how bookkeeping works, it's important to know what bookkeeping is.

Bookkeeping is the process of recording daily transactions and organizing financial documents. Accounting uses the data gleaned from bookkeeping records to make sense of a company's finances and progress. Simply put, a bookkeeper tracks finances and an accountant analyzes them.

Sounds easy, right? Bookkeeping is definitely less daunting when you know it doesn't require the same math ability as accountancy. Bookkeeping can be easy, as long as you're organized. It might seem like something you can handle yourself or something you'd rather outsource but either way, you should understand how it works. When bookkeeping, there are three main things you need to do:

1. Keep track of your finances

When bookkeeping for your small business, you can break down your finances into four categories: profits, expenses, inventory cycle, and liabilities. Profits can be divided into cash or credit sales, depending on whether the customer pays you at the time of purchase or when you send them a bill. Expenses can be divided into recurring or non-recurring expenses; non-recurring expenses are usually one-off unexpected payments, whereas recurring expenses cover items such as bills. If your business sells a product, your inventory cycle should catalogue product purchases and sales, allowing you to see how much inventory you have at all times. Liabilities are separate to expenses and should be organized accordingly. Liabilities are outstanding balances your company owes, as opposed to expenses that are incurred by the running of the business (such as buying inventory and paying employees).

2. Organize your accounts

Having properly organized accounts will make accounting easier and allow you to quickly and easily look over your finances at any time. If you are unsure how to organize your accounts and won't be handling the accounting yourself, talking to your accountant about what they need from you as the company's bookkeeper will help you to do your job properly. A general rule to follow when organizing your books is to divide things into the following categories; assets, liabilities, income, expenses, and equity. These categories will cover what the company owns and owes, as well as all the money going in and out of the business. By dividing your books like this, you and your accountant will be able to find the appropriate documents in record time.

3.   Regularly reconcile your books

How often you close and reconcile your books is a decision you will need to make with your accountant. An accounting period can be a month, a quarter, or a year, depending on what works best for your organization. When each accounting period ends, you will need to complete a series of bookkeeping tasks before the next period begins. These tasks include reconciling, which means checking that the company's bank and credit card statements match your books. A lot of these tasks are about making sure you can account for every cent that has gone in and out of the company. By doing these tasks regularly, you will be calm and prepared when it's time to file your taxes.

Bookkeeping is simply the organization of your company's finances. The key to great bookkeeping is regular, thorough analysis of your books. Bookkeeping shows you what's happening in your company, so a good way to know if you're doing things right is to ask yourself this- "Can I track every cent of the company's money right now?" When the answer is "yes", your books will be a great asset to you, your accountant, and the future of your business.

Chapter 2:
Bookkeeping Tools

Establishing advertising goals is critical to the success of your ad campaigns. Countless entrepreneurs and businesses have setup an advertising account, run a few ads, and then let it sit untouched for months or even years. This is usually due to a lack or absence of goals. So, before you even begin establishing any sort of advertising campaign or strategy, you need to establish clear advertising goals.

Even if you aren't a bookkeeping professional, it's important that you use professional-level tools. In this chapter, we're going to look at a few of the top bookkeeping software options on the market.

Remember, you want your bookkeeping software to be

- Easy to use
- Affordable
- Can be accessed by multiple company members

QuickBooks

QuickBooks by Intuit is the most popular option for small businesses when it comes to bookkeeping and accounting software. It is quite easy to use and can be integrated with a wide variety of external systems. QuickBooks has a mobile app where you can take photos of your receipts. Depending on which plan you choose, QuickBooks can cost between $15 and $35 per month. One, three or five people will be able to use your company's QuickBooks account together, based on your plan. This means you can easily share your books with your accountant, business partner, or anyone else who may need access.

Establishing advertising goals is critical to the success of your ad campaigns. Countless entrepreneurs and businesses have setup an advertising account, run a few ads, and then let it sit untouched for months or even years. This is usually due to a lack or absence of goals. So, before you even begin establishing any sort of advertising campaign or strategy, you need to establish clear advertising goals.

Even if you aren't a bookkeeping professional, it's important that you use professional-level tools. In this chapter, we're going to look at a few of the top bookkeeping software options on the market.

Remember, you want your bookkeeping software to be

- Easy to use
- Affordable
- Can be accessed by multiple company members

QuickBooks

QuickBooks by Intuit is the most popular option for small businesses when it comes to bookkeeping and accounting software. It is quite easy to use and can be integrated with a wide variety of external systems. QuickBooks has a mobile app where you can take photos of your receipts. Depending on which plan you choose, QuickBooks can cost between $15 and $35 per month. One, three or five people will be able to use your company's QuickBooks account together, based on your plan. This means you can easily share your books with your accountant, business partner, or anyone else who may need access.

Wave

Wave is a free bookkeeping and accounting program that was designed specifically for individuals and small businesses. It has a surprising amount of features for a free service such as tracking expenses, sending invoices, and balancing books. It can't do everything, but it's a great option if you're just starting out or trying to keep your budget tight. There's a premium option with even more features, which has the added bonus of removing the ads you'd receive in the free version. Wave also has a mobile app that allows you to take and store photos of your receipts.

Xero

Xero is another easy-to-use program, though some users feel that it's too basic and they spend a lot of money on add-ons to make up for the program's missing features. This program could work well for a small business, but you may need to switch to a more comprehensive program if your business grows larger. Xero has a mobile app and has no limit to how many company members can access one account. Depending on which plan you choose, Xero can cost between $9 and $180 per month.

Sage

Sage have a wide variety of programs, which they divide by the size of the customer's business. You can, of course, choose any of their options but their goal with these categories is to give you exactly what you need based on their experience with companies of a similar size. Their small business package (Sage Business Cloud) costs $10 per month and allows you to manage accounts, payroll, payments and books. With this package, the account can be accessed by as many company members as you'd like.

If this all seems overwhelming, keep in mind that you can get help and advice from a bookkeeper without hiring them full time. You can find a bookkeeper that will work with you once or a handful of times to look at your company, introduce you to some suitable options, and even show you how to use the software you choose. You may decide to have someone come in every month or every quarter to check that you're doing everything correctly or answer any questions you might have.

Chapter 3:

Hiring a Bookkeeper

For some people, hiring a bookkeeper is a necessary expense. You may want to delegate this work while you focus on other aspects of your company, but feel that you don't know enough about bookkeeping to hire the right person. In this chapter, you'll find a list of what you'll need from your bookkeeper and some helpful ways to hire the right candidate.

When starting a new business, you'll be trying to keep costs down wherever you can, so hiring someone to do something you could do yourself may seem counter-intuitive. However, a bookkeeper will save you time and money. You'll have more time to spend on building your business and following your passion, and save money by having a professional organize your finances from day one.

When considering someone as your company's bookkeeper, it's helpful to keep these things in mind:

- What kind of business do I run, and does my bookkeeper understand how books for this company will be different to businesses in other industries?
- What bookkeeping software does my bookkeeper recommend, and why?
- Is my business large enough to require a full-time bookkeeper, or would a part-time bookkeeper be better?

Asking a candidate (as well as yourself) these questions will allow you to see what this person would prioritize when working for you. If these priorities align with yours, then they could be a good fit for your business!

When hiring a bookkeeper, don't limit yourself to a person in your office space. There are so many bookkeeping options now, so don't be afraid to explore them! Bookkeeping firms and remote workers are both viable alternatives to a new employee- even if you aren't considering them, a little investigating might lead you to the perfect bookkeeper. As long as the person you hire has the right qualifications, the way you hire them won't matter.

As mentioned in Chapter Two, you might want to only bring in a bookkeeper to check the books every so often. This can save on costs while preventing oversights that you, as an inexperienced bookkeeper, might make. As you learn more about bookkeeping, you might call in your bookkeeper less frequently until you're able to do it all on your own. As a small business owner, you have the scope and power to decide what works best for you. You can try to do your own bookkeeping at first and then hire someone so you can focus on other things, or learn from a professional and take over when you feel confident.

Conclusion

The role of a bookkeeper is to keep track of finances, organize the accounts, and close and reconcile the books. The difference between a bookkeeper and an accountant is that a bookkeeper organizes a company's finances while an accountant uses them to see how well the company is doing and how they can grow.

If you're considering doing your own bookkeeping, there are dozens of online bookkeeping programs that can be used to organize and share finances within the company. QuickBooks, Wave, Xero, and Sage are all great options for small businesses, each with their own pros and cons. Make sure to check out their websites for more information and pricing options.

If you hire a bookkeeper for your business, make sure they understand the nuances of your business and can work with you through a good accounting program. Examine your business and decide if you need a full-time, part-time, consulting or remote bookkeeper. As a small business owner, you can be very flexible in this regard and this could give you an edge that saves you money and makes everything as easy as possible.

Deciding how to handle your company's bookkeeping can be very difficult when you're starting a business. The benefit of professional help against the detriment of additional cost is a struggle you will face at every turn. Whether you decide to do your own bookkeeping or hire a professional, you'll hopefully feel more confident about the importance of bookkeeping for your business after reading this book.